GOD AND MAMMON

CHAPTER I

To write is to hand oneself over. We do not realise this when writing our first book, and are therefore shocked by Claudel's epigram : " The man of letters—the assassin and the brothel child . . ."

It is not that a young author doubts that he is the material from which his book is moulded, but he believes that the object of art is to use the particular heaven and earth inside him in order to create new heavens and new earths whose original form will not be recognisable. He knows that he, the writer, is immanent in his work, and he faces the possibility that observant readers will discover him in what he has written ; but this does not worry him, as he also knows that only with sympathy and charity and love can the reader discover the real appearance of the author and distinguish it from a preconceived idea, just as only mystics can trace an image and a shadow of their God in the visible world.

It is true to say that as soon as an author

ceases to be content with actually depicting
reality but wants to give an impression of reality
—as soon as he ceases to be content with com-
municating facts but wants, rather, to express
his own feelings about facts—then he no longer
lays bare externals to the curious gaze of the
reader, but he lays bare, or gives up, himself.

The majority of modern readers want to find
the writer himself in his work. What Baudelaire
said in gentle insult to his reader, the contemporary reader returns to the author : " Hypocritical reader, my kindred spirit, my brother ..."
It is precisely a kindred spirit and a brother that
the reader is looking for in a book so that he
may be instructed as to what his own attitude
should be towards life and death. He is looking
less for principles than for a certain attitude.
Principles are found among the philosophers,
and the reader is usually a man who is ignorant
of anything outside what he can feel and touch—
he is out of his depth in abstractions and he cannot swim ; he should learn, yes, but the vocabulary
of philosophy puts him off, and, more difficult
still, the majority of philosophers depend largely
on allusion to things that have gone before—in
fact there is not a philosophical system in
existence which does not presuppose a knowledge
of what has gone before. Now, it is impossible
for the average reader to isolate one moment

6

from the stream of human thought, or to begin in the middle of the stream : philosophy is an endless web which has no seam and therefore no facility for random entry.

Moreover, time presses, and the point is to learn how to live. The difficulties which I must overcome are as particularly and uniquely mine as my features, and no general law has foreseen them. Thus, while philosophers deal with universals, every work of literature is a reflection of an individual. A literature is a collection of characters, and one book reflects a sensibility with special laws of its own. Therefore, it would be impossible for a reader not to find, among everyone who has written since writing began, a half-brother and a kindred spirit.

In epochs when Wisdom was a force in the world, writers as well as philosophers avoided the particular ; but the pagans of to-day hold no brief for the " man in general " of the classics. This conception held good during Christian eras when there was a universal acceptance of the moral law ; and thus literature had a universal value. The perverted and twisted type of man always escaped from the literary net ; he was a case for the confessor or the casuist, who swiftly related his actions to one of the seven capital sins and submitted them to existing sanctions.

According to Christian teaching, the great classics—even when salacious—distinguish good from evil, and judge man by this distinction. But now that we have reached the stage of abolishing God's truth within ourselves, and have overthrown what Bossuet called " the solemn tribunal of conscience which condemned all crimes " ; each literary man who comes along is equipped with his own universal remedy and thus assumes a special importance ; his head swells, and his prestige increases in proportion as his faith decreases.

The Christian distinction between good and evil obliged the writer to preserve a consistent criterion when considering human nature ; but now that that distinction has been discredited, everything can be questioned. There is no longer one truth, but as many truths as there are individuals. In the place of an examination of conscience which used to be pursued in the light of Christ—and which usually led to the abandoning or moderating or repressing of vicious tendencies—ill-judged leaders of contemporary thought have substituted an auto-creation which requires no moderation or repression of any sort.

So it is that works of art are becoming less and less objective—less and less detached from the artist—and as this happens in literature, more

8

and more does the public expect and provoke
the author to lay himself bare. It asks him about
his self-discoveries from the first moment of his
awareness. What obstacles did he have to overcome? Had he sexual difficulties? Did his
actions fit in with his desires? Did he relate his
personal requirements to the common good?
Has he still got a vestige of religion? If so, has
he absorbed it into his being, or does it tend to
hamper his self-realisation and self-expression?
However humble an author may be, and however
limited the field of his influence, he is perpetually being urged to unveil himself.

Our contemporaries, far more than the
Romantics, are the sons and heirs of Rousseau.
The Romantics were corrupt children of Christ,
and they held strongly to the old distinction
between good and evil, even though they exalted
evil and played the parts of fallen angels. To-day
there are many who force themselves to accept
themselves as they are, as Rousseau did. But
while Rousseau, imbued with moralism though
he was, failed to harmonise his interior self—
which he loved—with himself the social being,
modern writers are not concerned with the figure
they cut in the world, even if this figure, judged
by traditional standards, is perverted and twisted.
These writers are courageous in a way, though
not so courageous as they themselves think, for

9

first they hesitate, then they risk half-admissions, and then they draw back again before they finally take the plunge. They have to have the complicity and collaboration of their readers to brace them up, and they need admirers who demand from them an example, an authorization, and a justification.

A man who has lost the power of distinguishing between good and evil for himself pursues a desperate inquiry and research among writers. He is not satisfied merely with convincing himself that he is not a monster ; he wants to be reassured by finding someone like himself somewhere. He does not limit this inquiry to writers only. Since the war we have all become familiar with the young man who prowls around anxiously and inquisitively, searching for someone like himself. If he sees a connection between his own failures and the failures of the post-war generation, he tells himself that similar causes ought to produce similar failures in everyone of his generation. The passion for proselytism that can be observed among all the half-cracked people of recent years is really only a manifestation of an intense desire to be one of a number ; these people do not want to reform others, they want to persuade them that they are all the offspring of the same decadence and therefore are bound to have characteristics in common.

" You have no tail either," said the fox, whose tail had been cut off, to his companions, " you know very well you have not." When a writer is provoked in this way—however determined he may be not to give himself away—he is gradually and slowly and unwillingly forced to show his hand.

All his resolutions not to divulge those secrets that are his alone—for instance, his religious beliefs—are frustrated. Yet if his work shows preoccupation with religion he will at once find himself labelled : Catholic Novelist. At the same time, the free way in which he depicts life will shock the pious critics, and he will be tempted to exclaim in the event of an interview, " I am not what is called a Catholic novelist. . . ."— and that is all that is needed for him to be treated as a renegade. Then, surely, it is his duty to protest that he denies nothing of what will always be his faith and his hope, and thus he is committed to a line from which he will never, never deviate.

Unless a writer is sustained by a modicum of admiration and friendship he easily reaches a state of indifference—however sensitive he may be. It is so easy to persuade ourselves that people we do not like do not exist. Putting aside the people who are united with us because we love them, we could effortlessly and unthinkingly repeat the vow of the Roman Emperor : the rest of humanity has one anonymous and grinning head which we annihilate by our indifference.

But the danger comes when we start answering back to the least criticism. I am always infuriated by the impression of me that journalists get from my work, but if this impression shocks me, obviously I should try to find out why it should. It is useless for me to assure myself that the picture they draw of me has no relation to the reality ; this does not alter the fact of the picture's existence. It is as irrefutable as a photograph which the photographer touches up so that the client shall consent to be recognized. The point is : how great is the disparity between what I am and what I appear to be ? As soon as a writer yields to the temptation of trying to gauge this disparity he loses for ever that state of grace which is the state of indifference.

It is at this juncture that the importance of the critic—and especially the hostile critic— seems to me so great, for, henceforward, the writer is continually comparing what he is or believes he is with the picture that unsympathetic critics have drawn of him. I have to ask myself whether what I imagine to be a warped and deformed version of my real self is not an unexpected aspect of my real self which I should resign myself to and gradually accustom myself to.

An author is only half aware of what he dissimulates. He has secrets, tricks, subterfuges, which he more or less admits to himself. The instinct for disguise is strong in him. He is everywhere in his work, and at the same time nowhere. What he does not realise is that, seen from the outside, the very characteristics which seem to him unimportant become significant. We can only see the sitting-room from the corridor, and a writer is hardly ever in the sitting-room. He may want to reveal some characteristic without the public's noticing it, and he may succeed, but in revenge his critic may discover some characteristic which he has made no effort to conceal—perhaps because he thought it was so harmless, or because he did not realise it was there, or because he had not admitted to himself it was there. The personality that we try to be and that is witnessed to by the official acts of our life, our declarations of principle, our social standing and our domestic life, is perpetually in conflict with another personality which is vaguer and less defined— because we are always trying to keep it in the shadow—but whose contours and physiognomy become clear-cut and accentuated with time. This second personality is obstinate, and, as a result of the persistent and unflagging demands that are made on it, it eventually assumes a definite shape—definite and distinct and altogether detached from our " public " personality, yet bound to it by numberless bonds.

Both these aspects of our personality are reflected in our work, and together they create a third image which, owing to its two-fold origin and consequent inherent contradictions, irritates the conscientious critic intensely.

Many critics want to know something about the people they have to criticise ; they do not like writers that they cannot pigeon-hole. Also, every intelligent man as well as every critic wants to know something about the author whose book he is reading. The reader who is just a reader and nothing more is able to lose himself entirely in a book and be " carried away "—he asks for nothing in a story so long as it grips his imagination ; but this brand of reader is found only in the man-in-the-street and in the majority of women, and there is one kind of literature which benefits by him. In our childhood we were all simply readers and nothing more : at the time when we were carried away by the characters of Jules Verne our curiosity was not aroused about the personality of Jules Verne nor about his literary wiles and tactics.

But our own public is determined to scrutinise the pages of any book to discover information about its author. Perhaps this is the case less

with professional reviewers than with that super-
abundance of literary men who write literary
criticism. Our time is spent handing ourselves
over to each other. We know the details of the
harems in which we were brought up, and we
show the least offensive parts of them. We can
thank God that when even the subtlest artist
discusses another he rarely penetrates beneath
the surface because, at bottom, he is only
interested in himself. As for the professional
critics, most of them are even less dangerous.

With regard to some of them, we can say what
Malebranche said of his dog : " It does not
feel "—or rather we can say : " It does not feel
any more ! " There are a few exceptions like
Bidou, G. Marcel, Jaloux, Thibaudet, Fernan-
dez and Du Bos, but apart from these most of
the critics—sated as they are with all the new
books which they are forced to swallow—seem
the people least capable of judging the real
value and import of a book. The more distinguished critics have sufficient conscience to
deny themselves the pleasure of reviewing books
that they have no sympathy for and do not
understand, and they put aside the amusement
of tracing past and present influences : these
are the harmless critics. The others are interested
in analysing the author rather than the work :
they want to discover for example whether he is

right-wing or left-wing. This kind of reviewer is the most easily irritated because, although a book can no more kick against its label than a flower in a hot-house, the author himself can kick. As soon as he is denominated " radical " he publishes a book which causes scandal in the radical ranks. It is impossible to pigeon-hole him and shut him up in a camp ; he will always push shoots in the opposite camp. These contradictions infuriate the reviewer who clings to his tabulations and classifications ; he curses hybrid writers more particularly as he himself has not the inclination, and probably not the leisure, and certainly not the ability, to enter into their complexities ; thus he falls back on hasty judgments and superficial condemnations which exasperate the writer, though he feigns contempt.

Certainly the writer despises these reviewers, but he cannot prevent himself from thinking about them a great deal ; because even if the conclusions of so-and-so appear to him unjust and crude, he cannot say the same of the premises. Thus he is bound to be led back to his own profound interior contradictions. The silliest article has this in its favour : that it obliges the author to face up to this problem ; and we should not ask more of our judges than to be led back to confront our own difficulties.

If these critics were themselves cleverer, they would expend less time and energy on us for they would be less interested in us. André Gide, for example, is so interested in his own particular drama—to the extent of keeping a diary of his own intimate diaries—that when he became interested in me he attributed my religious difficulties to the fact that I had, as he puts it, to *ask permission* to write *Destins* while at the same time remaining a Catholic.[1] Can my unrest—

---

[1]   Paris. 7 *May*, 1928.
" My dear Mauriac,

" Perhaps it is not from you direct that I have received your *Jean Racine*, since it bears no dedication ; but anyway I thank you for having written it. It is really an admirable book, and that is a word I hardly ever use to describe modern productions. I am sure it is quite unnecessary for me to tell you how much I am moved by it ; you were kind enough to let it be seen that you thought of me now and again while writing it. Oh, how grateful I am that you have debunked a great man ;—anything is worth more than an idolatrous reputation. Leave Souday to talk about ' calumny ' ; but let us admit that Racine emerges terribly belittled from your hands. You show a greater advance here in your knowledge of mankind than perhaps in any of your novels, and I think I prefer the author of *Racine* to the disturbing author of *Destins*, even.

" May I make an observation ? You write (p. 132) that ' in spite of the fable, nothing is less criminal than the anxiety of Phèdre.' But, dear friend, even a watering-down of the incestuous nature of Phèdre's love (and I agree with you that it was not incestuous) cannot take away from the fact that it was adulterous. Is it this that you call, a little further on, ' ordinary love ' ? The ideas you develop at this point are very interesting and would be very right if they did not follow from a false datum.

" I wrote all this before I had finished the book. The last chapters are no less good, in fact perhaps they are the best— the cleverest, anyway. But the last one of all forces me to make some reservations. When you speak of my unrest there is a misapprehension ; my dear friend, the unrest is not on my side but on yours. It is exactly this that upset Claudel. I am not a tormented person, and I never realised it more than when reading your book. It is precisely your restlessness that is the this unrest which Gide flatters himself that he has not got (though in this he belittles himself : the day when Gide is no longer restless, who knows what will become of his corpse ?)—can my religious unrest be confused with the uneasiness of a man who is torn between God and Mammon and who claims to sacrifice none of the advantages of a writer while at the same time sacrificing none of the hopes of a Catholic ?

most Christian element in you. But, in spite of the involutions of your specious thought, the Catholic point of view of the ageing Racine and your point of view as a Catholic novelist differ to such an extent as to be positively opposed. Racine thanks God for His clemency in accepting him as His own *in spite of* his tragedies which he wished he had not written and which he talked of burning—for Racine understood much better than Massis the phrase which quite wrongly startled Massis : ' There is no such thing as a work of art written without the collaboration of the devil.' You, on the other hand, congratulate yourself that before Racine died God spared him the time to write his plays, and to write them *in spite of* his conversion. In fact, what you are searching for is the *permission* to write *Destins*—the *permission* to be a Catholic without having to burn your books ; and it is this that makes you write them in such a way that you will not have to disown them on account of your Catholicism. This reassuring compromise, which allows you to love God without losing sight of Mammon, causes you anguish of conscience and at the same time gives a great appeal to your face and great savour to your writings ; and it ought to delight those who, while abhorring sin, would hate not to be able to give a lot of thought to it. You know, moreover, what the effect would be on literature and especially on your own ; and you are not sufficiently Christian to cease to be a writer. Your particular art is to make accomplices of your readers. The object of your novels is not so much to bring sinners to Christianity as to remind Christians that there is something on earth besides heaven.

" Once I wrote—to the great indignation of certain people— ' It is fine sentiments that go to make bad literature.' Your literature is excellent, my dear Mauriac. Doubtless if I were more of a Christian I should be less your disciple.

" With all my friendship,

" André Gide."

Before we go further, we must realise that this question is not a simple one, and at least we ought to thank Gide and those other little lords whom we annoy so much for causing us to embark upon an examination of it. The question can no longer be ignored or avoided. We have lost the privilege of modesty and reserve ; writing is handing oneself over. However limited the circle of our readers may be, we have given them rights over us. There are Catholics who have faith in you, Mauriac, in spite of everything. Are they misled ? And others consider you a renegade. Are they mistaken ? Try to see the whole thing clearly. Try to map out your position *vis-à-vis* Catholicism and, please God, within Catholicism. It is not certain that you will be successful. If ever the title " Essay " could be justified, it would be justified for an inquiry like this.

CHAPTER II

A REMARK from Pascal throws light on the whole question. "It is useless for me to say: 'It must be admitted that the Christian religion has something astonishing in it'—people will answer: 'You think that because you were born in it.' Be that as it may, I myself harden myself against it precisely for that very reason— for fear lest my primary prejudice in its favour should undermine and seduce me. But even so, although I was born in it, I never cease to find it astonishing."

"Because you were born in it" . . . that is the drama of my life. I was born in it; I did not choose it; this religion has been imposed on me from the day of my birth. Many others have been born in it and have swiftly escaped from it; because the inoculation of the Faith did not *take* on them. But I belong to that race of people who, born in Catholicism, realise in earliest manhood that they will never be able to escape from it, will never be able to leave it or re-enter it. They were within it, they are within it, and they will be within it for ever and ever. They are inundated with light ; they know that it is true.

As soon as I understood that I could never abandon Catholicism, I let loose all my acutely critical inclinations and indulged them to the full ; this was my first sin, and I have paid dearly for it. All the difficulties and apparent impossibilities and superficial objections which I observed in my religious universe stuck in my throat. It is no exaggeration to say that from the age of sixteen I revolted against the pious practices of my family and masters and against the behaviour of the priests who came to our house. One of my school-friends who is now a priest could well describe my almost frenziedly-mocking attitude of those days. It was at that time that I read so much of Anatole France, and what I looked for particularly in his books were his caricatures of the clergy.

But the more I hammered against what I thought were bars, the more I found them unbreakable. I had not the power to lose my faith, even though I wanted to—for, secretly, I wanted to lose my faith in order to find it again. I knew even then that I was incapable of leaving Catholicism ; I was powerless against it ; it was there, in my innermost depths, and wherever I was, I knew my religion would be there too. Instead of accepting this grace as a grace, I

remember my envy one morning when I saw
Ernest Psichary in the Benedictine Nuns' chapel
in Paris. I looked upon him and Maritain as
the enviable elect—people for whom Catholicism
had been a *choice*, who had surveyed it from the
outside, who had turned it round and measured
it up and seen it in relationship to other religions.
Meanwhile I, who had never left it—who had
never been able to leave it—was perpetually
going from one extreme to the other, sometimes
imagining that Christianity was the sole preoccupation of the whole world and at other times
convinced that I was the prisoner of a little
Mediterranean sect. But for better or for worse,
I had to live in it ; I was incapable of not living
in it ; therefore, cost what it may, I had to adapt
myself to it. Thus at the age of sixteen I tried
desperately to prove to myself the truth of this
religion to which I was eternally bound. On
my table—as a witness to this adolescent obsession of mine—there lies a battered and very much
scribbled-over edition of Brunschvicg's *Pensées*.

During the first years of this century, the
Church in France went through a terrible crisis.
But the so-called lay laws in all their virulence
moved me less than the drama of Modernism.
In my ignorance I thought that the Church,
rejected by the modern world, was sulkily turning
her back on modern thoughts and ideas. I was

only a pretentious little ignoramus ; but the feverish excitement with which I lived through this drama gives me a feeling of tenderness even now when I recall it. The ancient and eternal ship withdrew itself from the world of men and plunged itself into confused darkness—but I was on board, I was a passenger, I was a part of it.

I loved it passionately and proudly, and never missed an opportunity of declaring my faith. I recollect one day at school, while I was doing my second year of philosophy : M. Drouin— our professor, and brother-in-law of André Gide—asked to be passed a manual for the next day's lesson, and I ostentatiously produced the absurd manual of a Father Lahr, which is used by the Marionites, and brought upon myself the jeers of the whole class.

This is not the place for me to go into the reasons as to why I was such fertile soil for Catholic culture ; it would involve too many explications of things extraneous to my immediate self—my family, for instance, and, above all, God's will towards me. But the fact is that I was so utterly devoted to God that, throughout my adolescence, all my worries and anxieties took the form of religious scruples ; everything centred round my ideas of purity, sin and the state of grace. More-over, I was very much moved by Huysmans at that time, and I loved the liturgy almost wildly,

23

and the music and—I hardly dare say it—the sacraments.

I must ask the Marionite fathers who educated me to forgive me if I affirm that, round about the year 1905, their religious instruction was practically non-existent ; it consisted of less than two hours a week, and neither the masters nor the boys attached much importance to it. I am certain that not one boy in my class would have known even broadly the sort of objections that a Catholic had to answer to during the first years of the century. On the other hand, however, the masters had perfected the art of surrounding us with an other-worldly atmosphere which infused holiness into every moment of the day : they formed not Catholic intelligences, but Catholic sensibilities.

I remember vividly the Sunday time-table : 7 o'clock, Communion Mass—9 o'clock, High Mass—10.30, Catechism and Congregation of the Blessed Virgin—1.30, Vespers and Benediction of the Blessed Sacrament. Doubtless many of us were to say later that we could dispense with church, having had enough of it at school to last a life-time ; but my temperament was very different—I was enraptured by everything in the liturgy and by even the simplest hymns. Exquisite or commonplace, this wine always made me drunk ; but even while at the heights of this drunkenness, the knowledge that I had not *chosen* it haunted me.

I remember how important I considered the successive conversions of Pascal to be, and I assured myself that it was possible to convert oneself inside Christianity. Once I said as a joke to a friend who felt the way I did about these things : " It was between my second and my third conversion." But above all I liked to be persuaded by Pascal that a search was always possible, that there could always be a voyage of discovery within revealed truth. And it was there that I joined hands with the Modernist unrest—though it was only an emotional attitude of my mind as my ignorance about philosophy was still very great.

Gradually I got used to the idea of being a Catholic for all eternity : I no longer hammered against the bars. The easy delights of a religious sensibility dictated *Les Mains Jointes* to me. I entered into literature a cherub of the sacristy, playing my little organ. If Barrès was moved by this dim hymn of mine it was because, in his magical perceptiveness, he discovered in it " a mad note of voluptuousness "—as he wrote in an article in the *Echo de Paris*.

I cultivated my garden, my monastery garden. I pretended to cultivate it, I played with the altar plate and sniffed the incense, but even then

I felt a secret disgust for this sensual devotion which I felt was the monopoly of people too cowardly to take risks. I was lost in the depths of what is called " Spiritual " literature,[1] but even so the terrible stark demands of Christianity were clear to me. I knew that the Christian God demanded everything. I knew that He had no part in the flesh and that the world of nature and the world of grace were two and inimical. Pascal taught me this with an almost excessive ruthlessness, and I knew it to be terrifyingly true.

At this time, however, and under cover of my pious airs and graces as a dutiful student, a powerful stream began to spring in me. At first it was only a trickle ; then I saw it rise and begin to overflow my thoughts, words and deeds. A sombre and powerful river now engulfed me. I discovered that I was as passionate as any other boy of my age. Twenty pious years had been able to do literally no more than delay the tide. It was as if my family and my masters had piled up stones over the source only to force the water to push a way of its own. Nature slowly gained the ascendancy over grace. I despaired of re-establishing a balance between them, and I saw these two enemy powers arrayed irrevocably

---

[1] I understand by that a sort of sugary and drawing-room æstheticism. But I came across admirable people and poets like my dear friend André Lafond and the fervent Robert Vallery-Radot, and Eusebe de Bremond d'Ars, etc.

one against the other. My God did not want me
to let my thoughts dwell, even for a moment,
on what my passions dictated. Then who, who
(an evil spirit whispered to me), who of the
people around me practised this pitiless, merciless
doctrine? Hardly anybody; and several people
who did, several people who had embraced the
folly of the cross, I found dying of thirst by the
very water which is supposed to quench all
thirst; and other adherents who were satisfied
I explained away by saying that they had never
felt any thirst. To-day, having arrived at an
age from which I can measure with a glance the
long road which I have traversed, I realise that
the reason why I have known people who have
lost their faith is because a troubled conscience
like mine finds satisfaction in trouble and thus
attracts and seeks out similar sorts of consciences.
A secret instinct turned me aside from people
who might have helped me to a vision of blessed
joy—a secret instinct, or rather, my perverted
will; for when the devil has his eye on someone,
he fears nothing more than that he should meet a
saint.

Nevertheless, I did not ever ask myself if the
moment had come for me to abandon Christianity. That did not enter into the question at
all. One issue alone agonized me: I had to
resolve it either by giving myself over to God or

to the devil. There was no hope of escaping from the Christian grip ; no possibility of abandoning the Christian scheme of things. If I had been able to do that, everything would probably have been solved. Others round about me went off on tip-toe or banged the door, and then re-made themselves according to another moral system. But for myself, I remained attached to the Church as narrowly as a man to this planet ; fleeing from it would have been as mad as trying to flee from this planet.

Nothing is more foreign to me than the outlook of those people who think that they can adapt Christianity to suit themselves, or rather, to suit their passions. They seize upon texts and twist them to fit their purposes. They can say what they like, but some of their works are the most undermining and the most dangerous variations of the gospel that a Christian has ever dared to attempt. When I was twenty I knew—without any merit on my part—that God would not allow my conscience to be thus deceived. However much the scrupulously-exact scales have been weighed down by my impulsive actions, the needle has always marked implacably the name and the gravity of my sins. Why reason it out and talk about it ? I knew what God's requirements were : His wish to be loved, and, what is much more important, His wish to be alone loved, or,

28

at any rate, His desire that we should not love anybody except for Him and in Him. And this does not destroy human love ; rather it makes it sublime.

All I could do was to throw myself headlong into literary work—to express and make palpable this monster that I could not conquer. My future work took shape and form in my eyes. But then I was assailed by a difficulty of another sort. The Catholic label brought my first attempts before some good people, but they—my books— were already giving cause for complaint. They were harmless enough and they did not shock timorous people, as I thought they might, but people who detected in them my secret difficulties and my secret monster. The conflict between the disinterestedness of the artist and what I called the utility-sense of the apostles soon broke out in me—an antagonism which I then thought unconquerable, but which to-day I hope to surmount. It is true that the defender of a sacred cause, the soldier of God, demands that everyone should serve, and by serve he often means : write nothing which is not immediately useful. " What is the use of that ? " he will ask about a novel. What I understood at that time by the " disinterestedness " of an artist was obviously inconceivable to such a man ; and when some people try to show him by famous examples that such uselessness is only apparent, and that a humanity deprived of Shakespeare, Racine and Dostoievsky would be infinitely impoverished, he replies : " You are neither Shakespeare nor Racine." Nevertheless, the humblest of us is convinced that he has the right to the title of artist so long as he undertakes his work in a spirit of purity and detachment and indifference to everything else. But the active Christian takes no notice of the innocence and candour of a writer if, as a writer, he is corrupt. There is no need to press this point here, as I am dealing with it at length in Chapter V. But the strange thing is that, faced with this issue, I have never thought of evading it for the sake of having peaceful elbow-room. I have frequently taken the part of my enemy-confrères against myself, because if I can forgive a work of art for being apparently useless, I cannot forgive it for being virulent and violent. Merely to speak of a soul in danger has always been enough to shatter me.

So I continued to work within the borders of Catholicism—an object of mistrust and even of contempt and reprobation to my fellow-Catholics. It seemed to me that they accepted me as one of them for the sole purpose of being able to judge and condemn me. And, what was worse, I regarded some of my judges with an atrocious ill-will. I ended up by deciding that there was a certain sort of stupidity and lying peculiar to them : they had the monopoly of a particular brand of unworthiness. I am going to make a clean breast of all my feelings about them : even at the height of my exasperation and at the worst moment of my revolt I never ceased to believe, or rather to see, something which hit my eyes—namely, that Catholicism arouses in human beings something which no other creed has ever aroused in them. I was always amazed by the fact that the common crowd in the street could walk carelessly past the shabby black cart and old horse of the Little Sisters of the Poor drawn up beside the pavement. I thank God that I have never ceased to venerate the heroes and saints who continue to testify to the Church ; but it is not against them that the unfortunate writer comes up. Let us admit that his pious opponents from the *bonne presse* sometimes distil a poison whose recipe I thought I had discovered : these people, I told myself, allow themselves to do anything so long as, judged by their own standards, it does not necessitate their going to confession. I said to myself : " If only that would take them just too far ! "—but that was only a clever ruse on my part because I knew that Christ, being Justice, hated injustice ; and everything condemned by reason in the world is

already condemned by God from all eternity.
But *was* Catholic criticism deeply unjust towards
my books? It certainly detected an element of
corruption in them; but am I sure that I, too,
cannot detect that element prowling over my
work, in the way it prowls over cemeteries which
are nevertheless dominated by the Cross?

However hostile I may have been to my co-
religionists, at least I have never blasphemed
against the eternal Church; but I said this to
myself: that if this Mother of humanity does love
humanity, ephermal human beings are certainly
not on the first rung of her heart. In her eyes, I
told myself, individuals are as dust and that is
why this Mother can sometimes seem to lack
flesh and blood: at the same time I beheld
myself inevitably in her hands. I could never
make an appeal against her sentence if she ever
struck me. I cannot leave the Church; the
threads of her net will not give way. If I tried
to escape, I should find her elsewhere. In this
sense I can claim that the Kingdom of God is
within me, and that " Rome is wherever I am."

People will probably say that I have no reason
to be surprised by this, and that I must study an
aspect of the phenomenon that is called, by
M. Estaunié, the Imprint. The power of religion
has been strengthened in me, they will say, by
my own weakness; my story is the story of all

weak souls, namely that I have offered fertile
soil for the cultivation of the faith. . . . No ;
it is not so simple as all that. To begin with,
not one of the infatuations which I have gone
through has escaped my present analysis. I
always put myself on guard against the æsthetic
side of present-day Catholicism, and its emotional
appeal, however sublime, at once excites my
mistrust. I long with all my soul for the " con-
solations of religion," but I know at what price
they must be bought. I know all about peace
in suffering, and I know that bitterness with
which past sins penetrate through present grace.

The tide of an ocean moves and agitates a
river long before the river's mouth, and in the
same way death is mingled with every Christian
life long before it is near. It is a basic instinct
in man to be horrified by the thought of his future
corpse, and in me this instinct goes very deep ;
and I have a whole set of other difficulties, too,
which it is not worth going into, as I know so
ridiculously little about science and philosophy.
Nevertheless, I shall just outline what, in speaking of Renan, M. Pierre Lasserre called " the
drama of Christian metaphysics," for this
" drama " was unfolded before me, too, though
in a coarser form. This is what happened : the
anchor was lifted, the hawsers were released, and
yet the ship hardly moved and the tide refused

to carry it along. In the middle of the terrible garden whose fences seemed broken down, the torn soul remained, riveted to the spot. It was separated from the other souls, but it remained there, still.

People will say : It is the old fear—it is the fear of the gods which has caused the gods to be created—the hideous fear that outlives faith even. Am I a creature who has been, since childhood, inveigled into adoration by fear ? Remember, Mauriac : the God of your childhood Who ruled in your home did not only control your least movements and your most secret and transitory thoughts, but He entered into the minutest details of your food. On Good Friday you had to be careful that the crust of your four o'clock roll was not " yellowed "— for eggs were forbidden even to children ; you had to take care that you did not swallow any water while doing your teeth or your Communion would be a sacrilege. You knew your soul much better than you knew your body. Are you quite sure that the God of your childhood who took such pleasure in details is not still spying on you in the dark ? I do not disown this God. I agree that I have exaggerated a little, but exaggerations are in the tradition of all Christian education. No confessor would blame this excess of prudence. The teaching of purity has no use for half-measures. " I want to be ignorant ; I want to be like a child in certain things," wrote the Abbé Perreyve on the eve of his ordination. You must have the courage to admit that, when you replace this " busy-body God " by a God who does not look at things with such minute care, you make no spiritual progress, but rather you decline spiritually. You become less scrupulous as you become less pure. You were taught from the age of reason that it was the true Christian law to make no concessions to the flesh. " In this matter, everything is serious," our teachers often used to say. Everything is serious ; everything involves eternity. And experience is the proof of our teachers' rightness. It is the soul that attains to God, and the flesh, when too much gratified, that separates us from Him infinitely. These unimaginable precautions are in conformity with the essential element in Christianity. When the real Christian re-awakes in you it is really your young self that is re-awakening in you—that self whose conscience was desperately frightened at the slightest taint ; and then this self comes up against the man you have since become, and the contrast between the two causes anguish. And it is acuter anguish still to feel that you can never get back to the source, never recapture the simplicity of your first beginnings.

c ɛ

None of this, however, has anything to do with the lesser agony of doubt. Doubt is nothing but a trivial agitation on the surface of the soul, while deep down there is a calm certainty. And however much this basic calm may be spattered by the mud of sentimental doubts, it can not be corroded ; it always stands firm.

It is difficult to define this incorruptible element in our faith. It is evident—and its evidence is the Cross. We have only to open our eyes to find it beside us—*our* cross which is waiting for us. Who would have imagined that two pieces of wood placed one upon the other could assume as many shapes as there are individual destinies ! And yet such is the case. Your cross is made to your measure, and you must stretch yourself out on it whether you want to or not, whether with hatred and revolt or with submission and love. It is a mystery that man should have lived for so long without discovering that, above life's charnel-house, there was a sign, a leafless tree, a naked tree on which, one day in human history, God Himself came to die. " O God, You have such tenderness and love for bodies in pain that You have chosen for Yourself the body most overwhelmed with suffering that has ever existed on earth . . ."

And even if our weakened and impoverished

faith can perceive the supernatural only from afar, we still have this wood to touch—this wood on which our flesh is nailed. The elements which make up each cross are a common heritage. I never understood the terrible cry of Michelet, quoted by Daniel Halévy : " . . . entering upon the great agony which is called old age . . ." Old age ! Long before we reach it we all breathe the breath of death ; but there is more agony than this, for above the base of communal pain there is each man's individual pain, the pain which corresponds to his heart and is measured with his body and which has no resemblance to any other pain. It is the privilege of artists to describe their pain in its details and its differences, and it is this that creates the particular style of each and gives to each his particular distinction.

The Cross ! I cannot escape from it. " If Thou art the Son of God," cried the insulters of Christ Crucified, " come down from Thy cross." He could have if He had wanted to. But as for us, His creatures, nothing can tear us from this gibbet on which we were born, which has grown side by side with our bodies and stretched itself with the stretching of our limbs. We are hardly conscious of it in our youth, but as the body develops and grows, the flesh becomes heavy and drags on the nails. What a time it takes for us to realise that we are born crucified!

This soul I am describing is on a lower level than even the worst souls because this soul is aware and the others are not. Nevertheless it preserves, in the midst of their " Walpurgis night," a sharp clarity of vision. The cross of the others is as visible to it as its own, and this cross appears abandoned, misunderstood, unknown. All these other destinies, spread out and unloosened seemingly haphazardly, are unaware of their centre—that centre which would infuse them with order. To flee one's sorrow and evade and ignore one's cross is the whole occupation of the world ; but that occupation is at the same time a fleeing from one's own self and a losing of one's own self, for our special aspect is given us by our sorrow and our special contours are fixed and checked by our cross.

I am not obsessed now, as I used to be, by the small place that Christianity occupies in the world. Outside the mystical city of those who know their cross and hence know themselves— who bear their cross and hence support them- selves—there swarms the mass of people bent on ignoring, losing, annihilating themselves. I detest the look of an Arab or a Hindoo or a Chinaman because I detect in it at once the absence of the cross, the sought-out, pursued and wished-for ignorance of individual suffering. They throw off this bracing support that Christ gives us every time it is renewed until they rid themselves of it entirely. Although this gibbet stands poised over emptiness they wrench themselves from it and fall downwards with delight. The thing that gives such tragedy to the mania for drugs is the fact that they offer, in dreams, an opportunity for fleeing from the cross. Opium is the frontier traversed by deserters from the cross and beyond which they find nothing but the mockery of a substitute for the only Peace : " Pax Dei quae exsuperat omne sensum. . . ." (St. Paul to the Philippians).

What does it mean to lose one's faith ? I see what I am telling you, and I cannot help seeing it. Those born Christians who separate themselves from their faith and live in peace after the separation have never apprehended the fact of the cross.

We are born the prisoner of our cross. Nothing can tear us from it. But it is peculiar to the Christians of my country to believe that they can come down from their cross. And in fact they do come down from it. Thus much are they free : they can refuse the cross. They go away from it, lose awareness of the mysterious thread which binds them to it and which they stretch so excessively that if ever they turn back they can no longer see the fateful sign in the sky. They go on and on until, stopped by an obstacle and suffering from a wound in the heart, they stumble and give in. Then, however utterly they may have been lost, once again the bonds draw them back with a surprising force, and once again they are mercifully hurled against the wood. As by instinct they stretch out their arms and offer their hands and feet, already pierced from childhood.

CHAPTER III

Now imagine a human being who has great powers of resistance, who is much more masterful than I am, and who hates this servitude. Imagine a nature irritated and exasperated to distraction by this mysterious servitude and finally delivered over to an abandoned hatred of the cross. He spits on this sign which he drags after him and assures himself that the bonds which attach him to it could never stand out against a methodical and planned degradation of his soul and spirit. Thus he cultivates blasphemy and perfects it as an art and fortifies his hatred of sacred things with an armour of scornful contempt. Then suddenly, above this stupendous defilement, a voice rises, complainingly, appealingly ; it is hardly so much as a cry, and no sooner has the sky received it than the echo is smothered by frightful jeers and by the laugh of the devil. As long as this man is strong enough, he will drag this cross as a prisoner his ball-chain, never accepting it. He will obstinately insist on wearing this wood along all the paths of the world. He

41

will choose the lands of fire and ashes most suited to consume it. However heavy the cross becomes, it will not exhaust his hatred—until the fateful day, the turning-point in his destiny, when he sinks down at last under the weight of the tree and under its agonizing embrace. He still writhes, pulls himself together and then sinks down again, hurling out a last blasphemy. From his hospital bed he brings abominable accusations against the nuns who are tending him ; he treats the angelic sister as a fool and an idiot and then, at last, he breaks off. This is the moment marked from all eternity. The cross which has dragged after him for thirty-seven years and which he has denied and covered with spittle offers its arms to him : the dying man throws himself upon it, presses it to him, clings to it, embraces it ; he is serenely sad and heaven is in his eyes. His voice is heard : " Everything must be prepared in my room, everything must be arranged. The chaplain will come back with the Sacraments. You will see. They're going to bring the candles and the lace. There must be white linen everywhere. . . ."

That is the mystery of Arthur Rimbaud. He was not only that wild-looking mystic seen by Claudel nor yet that gutter-snipe genius who is taken up by the young sensualists of to-day. He was a man crucified in spite of himself, who hated his cross and was tormented by it ; and he suffered anguish in allowing it to win.

If we want to understand Rimbaud we must understand his terrible mother, " mother Rimb." She was a Christian and she willed, with a will of iron, that her children should be Christians. Arthur, for better or for worse, was one. He sweated obedience, as he said. Every Sunday, pomaded and good as gold, the little boy sat at a mahogany loo-table reading the Bible. Was he a hypocrite ? Remember his holy fury when he saw some college boys laughing round a holy-water font : he threw himself on them with all the force of his young being. But certainly he would have been glad to escape from the rule of the Church which he had not chosen and which he therefore cursed. *Une Saison en Enfer* shows both his subjection and his hatred. He hates the yoke and yet the yoke is upon him. Rimbaud's blasphemy exceeds all bounds because it is deliberate yet torn from his throat as if with difficulty. The note that springs from his very essence, naturally and inevitably, is the note which is, as Claudel says, " of the purity of Paradise, of infinite sweetness, of heart-breaking sadness." What he fails to say is that Rimbaud's heart has received the imprint of grace and that he hears the rational singing of the angels : " Reason is born in me, the world is good, I will

bless life and love my sons. . . ." Then, stupi-
fied by this unknown purity which presents
itself in him—as if coming from someone else—
he revolts against it and blasphemes Christ
terribly. Remember how he walked about
London, drunken and criminal-looking. And
after having scared Verlaine mortally he declaims,
and speaks to him in tender *patois* " of death
which brings repentance, of wretched people who
certainly exist, of painful toil and of separations
which tear hearts in two. In the dens where we
got drunk he cried thinking of the people around
us, human cattle of misery. He picked up the
drunkards in the dark streets. . . ."

Nevertheless, it was Christ Himself that he
pursued with such hatred in Verlaine who had
returned to God. When Verlaine arranged to
meet him in Germany, Rimbaud saw him coming
" with a rosary in his claws " in order to convert
him. Thus he derived infinite pleasure in getting
poor Verlaine drunk and making him renounce
God, Our Lady and the saints. And on another
occasion he threw himself on him and hit him
like a madman. But beyond Verlaine's lament-
able face which he bruised and wounded, did not
he discern Another? Did not he recognise the
sweat of blood and the expression of suffering and
love? Similarly, was not it a voice other than
Verlaine's which he heard in the poems of

Sagesse—sent to him by his friend when he was at Roche ? But it was in the lavatory that Isabelle found the manuscript. Rimbaud was determined to dishonour in Verlaine the living Christ.

From the youthful day when, ashamed of having spoken and having betrayed himself, he vowed himself to silence, until his death agony, when he was surrounded by angels, can we find one single sign of the presence and of the unconquerable possession of Christ ? Only one phrase, a single phrase in a letter to his mother from Harrar on May 25th, 1881 : " If I am forced to go on wearying myself as at present, and to feed myself on chagrins which are as violent as they are absurd, in vile climates, I fear I may cut short my existence. . . . Could we but enjoy a few years of real rest in this life ! Happily this life is the only one : which is obvious because one cannot imagine another life with more boredom in it than this one."

Young Rimbaud had burnt his manuscripts and chosen to remain silent for always. But this little phrase in a hasty letter is enough for one to hear the groaning of an entrapped soul. If ever human words meant the opposite of what they appear to mean, this furious affirmation does : " Happily this life is the only one. . . ."

Then the current of grace was lost once again and only burst forth in the last days of his life,

45

on his hospital bed. You may say that terror removes all importance from these death-bed conversions. But one must remember the astonishment of the chaplain after he had confessed Rimbaud : not only had the dying man the faith, but, according to the chaplain, this faith was of a very rare quality—a quality which he had hardly ever met with before.

CHAPTER IV

THERE is a certain sickness that the eldest son and the worker of the first hour have in common.

Whatever the eldest son may do, he can never return home because he has never gone away from home. He can never see his Father's house from the outside ; he cannot measure its solidity or gauge the place that it occupies in the world. Through having received his Father's love habitually, he runs the risk of never feeling its consolation again, and he has taken his place at table so often that he does not notice the taste of the bread and the wine any more.

The case is the same for the worker of the first hour. He does not feel any joy in his work nor any eagerness in the achievement of it. He does not know why he began work at all, yet he will not go on strike because he cannot leave his job before he has got his wages. He is not helped along by love because he and the Master know each other too well, he says to himself; they do not even see each other any more. The worker of the first hour is deceitful, and he does as little as possible knowing that he will be paid along with the others at the end.

And even the prodigal Son and the lost Sheep could be prodigal and lost, the first, only in his father's house, and the second, only in its native pastures. When they both thought that they had strayed a long way and seen strange lands, they discovered that they had only turned round in a circle and floundered in the same place.

The power of religion on someone who believes in religion is the same as this. Everything is concentrated in religion—even things that seem to be at its opposite pole. A convinced Catholic is incapable of making a gesture to set himself free because any gesture will assume some significance in the religious scheme. Of course he may escape from grace—but falling into sin is not escaping from Christianity ; on the contrary, it may even be an inexorable bond to Christianity. In the case of a Catholic like this, yielding to his passions and pandering to his doubts by supporting them with all sorts of doctrines—and even sacrificing to idols—does not in any way presuppose the abandonment of Christianity. Péguy wrote : " The sinner belongs to Christianity. The sinner can pray the best prayer. . . . The sinner is an integral part, an integral factor, in the mechanism of Christianity. The sinner is at the very heart of Christianity.

. . . The sinner and the saint are equally integral parts in the make-up of Christianity. They are each equally indispensable to the other, and both are indispensable to Christianity. The one and the other form two complementary and uninterchangeable—yet with each other interchangeable—parts of the unique mechanism which is the mechanism of Christianity."

There is a type of man who, once inserted in this mechanism, will never leave it. The only exit, sin, is no exit for him ; it is a door which does not open on to the outside. He has the power of passing from Grace to sin and from sin to Grace ; he is free to bear witness or not to bear witness. Neither doubt nor negation nor even renunciation can tear off this garment which is glued to his skin.

Thus I am a long way from " that reassuring compromise which allows me to love God without losing sight of Mammon." If I refuse to accept this reproach of Gide's it is not because I think I am innocent. I am probably more guilty than a man who is tugged both ways, who wants to write his books without missing heaven and to win heaven without foregoing his books. It is putting it much too mildly to say that I " do not lose sight of Mammon." The fact is that I am in the front line of his besiegers. But the impossibility of serving two masters does not necessarily mean the forsaking of one for the other to the extent of losing sight of the forsaken One or losing awareness of His presence and power. And even if this sight and awareness were lost, we would still be wearing the untearable livery of the Master we had betrayed ; we would still, by force or by free will, belong to His house ; we would still carry His mysterious arms wherever we went. However far we might stray, there would always be someone to say : " But you, you also were with this Man—you were among those who followed this Man."

Our most free writings will always bear a certain mark, a certain stamp, a taste of the earth—of the earth where the vines and the corn contained infinitely more, potentially, than our daily bread and wine.

Is this sort of writer a prisoner ? If he is, he is a prisoner who refuses to ask pity from the world because he does not deserve the pity of the world. If this fate seems terrible, it is so only on the supernatural plane. The drama of life for this kind of writer is real only if the universe and his destiny have one and the same direction and end. His first preoccupation is his salvation. It always seems strange to me that people who deny salvation and believe only in what they see should pity this kind of writer. If his fellow-believers who care about him have reason to be alarmed about him, it would be much more sensible for unbelievers to envy him since they know, especially if they are professional writers, what a great danger complete liberty can be.

Look at them ! They are all searching for a datum, a scale of values. I am not speaking of philosophers, who have their criteria, but of writers—or any artists—who stake all they have got on sentiments and sensations. Tottering worlds, confused forces, destroyings and dispersings, and then—the fitting conclusion—nothingness ! They are haunted by nothingness. The public life of Barrès, his political attitude, the League of Patriots, the Chamber of Deputies, the *Echo de Paris*—these were all defences against nothingness. He put the Palais-Bourbon between himself and nothingness.

Then turn and look at the children of this pathetic century ! The names of two books, taken at random from among the best productions of recent years, bear painful witness to their restless disorder. *Rien que la Terre*, cries the first : *Voyageurs traqués* (entrapped), answers the second. Nothing but the world, nothing but that—for people who live with their senses only. The old planet is soon crossed, the fruit is soon peeled and squeezed and thrown away. In the second book a man is searching for *supports*. He leaves school, goes through the war, then through sport, then through bull-fighting . . . then what? The continents of the world sent him bounding off them like a rubber ball.

It is a great mistake to think that a bad Catholic is in any way triumphant or thinks himself stronger than other men. With him, first of all, everything falls into place and into a category of values ; the least sensation finds its niche. All his human loves form a block which is arrayed against the unique Love. He does not yield to desires, pleasures or pain without having in mind a statue of himself and contributing somehow to its formation. The slightest touch counts ; all the time the statue is taking shape ; everything he does adds something to its moulding, and it is watched with censure or with love by the Almighty.

The sceptic says to the Catholic writer : " Certainly you can withhold your values because they are negligible for a writer. But what advantages have you got outside literature ? ' Nothing but the world ' is certainly sad, but ' Nothing but heaven ' is useless to a halting and hesitating Catholic who has lost both the desire and the will to renounce ephemeral things."

The transitory here-and-now is perhaps the most important obsession which a bad Catholic can have, and he owes it to his long familiarity with the supernatural. When he was young he trembled with fear at retreats preached by priests who enjoy giving children a whiff of their future corpses. These priests were too simple or too pure to realise that a boy is attracted by ephemeral things precisely because they are ephemeral. They could never succeed in deflecting a boy from his love of the transitory—rather, they could only make this love the more desperate by bringing it home to him.

The sceptic pities the indifferent Catholic most of all for having to renounce the morality—if so it can be called—which gives man the illusion of ennobling his youth without depriving it of its joy (an ethic formulated, before Nietzsche, by Stendhal). The Christian, however, knows that this "morality" is valid only for young people who do not care about metaphysics and who do not turn cold at the thought of death. It is a morality adapted only to youth. It owes both its charm and its weakness to the fact that it concerns one moment of life only—that moment when the force of our blood deludes us into thinking that all power and domination is ours, that we are the chosen of the earth, and that we shall live for ever.

I do not mean that Julien Sorel and Fabrice [1] never think about death ; but they think of it as a risk that they can run or not run, a risk that

---

[1] Two of Stendhal's characters.

it is honourable to run for love or even for fun. Everything belongs to youth, or so youth believes, even death. The idea of suicide occurs to the young more than to the old because the young look on death as a choice and they think they are free not to die. With the turn of the years half-way along the road of life death loses its glamour and ceases to be the stake for love and happiness. Instead, it becomes an inevitable door that opens into obscurity. One can still boast one's strength, clench one's fists and proclaim oneself master and lord—but such bravado has become a hollow sham. The trembling of the sceptic before this unexplored darkness is surely worth less than the trembling of the believer whose fear is at least mingled with love or the beginnings of love.

The opponent of Christianity will insist that the sceptic's youthful illusions are an advantage. During his adolescence he has not been paralysed with the thought of death, and he has been able to concentrate on acquiring human and worldly virtues such as fortitude, courage, boldness, the taste for victory in love, the pride of power. He intends to compensate for " the frightful punishment called old age " by living dangerously while he can, risking everything at every moment purely for the sake of feeling his heart beat more quickly. A past of this kind is a consolation to

54

an ageing sceptic or sensualist who is condemned
to death and who has lost the power to live the
life which is also lost.

We are all condemned to death, but the sceptic
is not condemned until he has reached old age,
whereas the Catholic is condemned from his
childhood. Ever since I was ten I have been
bowed down under the inheritance of *Eccle-
siastes*. But a child with an heroic spirit can use
the virtues that I have called " human " on the
Christian plane. Christ has great need for bold
advocates of His cause. The saints had domination over men. The transient conquests of
Alexander and Bonaparte do not bare com-
parison with the victories of St. Francis and St.
Theresa and their mystical empire which has
conquered time. " To live dangerously " is a
Christian formula, and assumes its deepest
meaning on the supernatural plane.

But this, alas, is tantamount to saying that
Christianity cannot tolerate mediocre souls. A
mediocre sceptic can follow Beyle's advice and
live a decorative life, satisfy his refined tastes
in moderation, be honourable according to the
world's standard of honour, and altogether earn
praise for having a charming character. But a
mediocre Christian preserves only the negative
element in Christianity—he refrains from doing
forbidden things and is always in a position of

retreat or refusal : if he is guilty he hides and puts you on the wrong scent—practised as he is in the art of playing a part. One man is happy— the man who can cross the abyss with one leap and land on the other side a saint. The half-way position is valueless. The world is justified in eschewing Christians who are Christians in spite of themselves, but it is unaware of their tragedy which is the tragedy of not being able to choose : they are embogged half-way up Mount Tabor, incapable of advancing or escaping.

A man may have the misfortune to be imprisoned in a metaphysic which he disagrees with body and soul ; but if he has, at the same time, the supreme good fortune of being able to express himself, his work will help to occupy him and fill his life. He will persuade himself that an artist does not need to possess a domain but merely a little corner. Alfred de Vigny says that mankind carries on an endless conversation in which each man of genius represents an idea. In reality a conversation is made up of general ideas—but in them there are millions of nuances, and it is the business of writers to express these nuances. The vast works of Pascal, Rousseau, Chateaubriand and Barrès leave ample room for this kind of small and subtle, almost underhand variation.

We must record our personal drama exactly

as it is ; we must hand ourselves over—but in an artistic way. It is not ourselves that matter, but our work whose material we are.

Who is this new God whose prerogatives I do not dispute and to whom I owe everything ? Did I ask for, or receive from anyone, " the *permission* to write *Destins* "—as Gide puts it ? How did I come to contemplate such an infringement of my liberty, such a dependence ?

I must not make the denial that Cain made. Yes ; I am my brother's keeper. I do not want to die before I have written the drama of the world and its creatures as I have seen it in my life. I want to leave an account of my personal vision behind me, fixed in the minds of the greatest possible number of people. I want to reach and touch as many people as possible. But touching means wounding. Books are violent things—violations sometimes—and they pierce some hearts deeply. (I remember all the letters I received after I wrote *Souffrances du Chrétien* in the *Nouvelle Revue Française*—and I only wanted to persuade people that my religion was both true and impracticable—so as to excuse my own powerlessness to conform my life to it !) There is no question nearer to my heart than that of the intense responsibility of being a writer.

CHAPTER V [1]

For many writers this question does not so much as arise. If there is one dogma which has gained the support of the majority of writers in this century and the last, it is the dogma of the absolute independence of the artist. It seems to be agreed, once and for all, that a work of art has no object outside itself. It only counts in so far as it is gratuitous or useless : anything written to prove a point or to be of use is disqualified from the realm of art. Gide says that " the moral issue for the artist is not that he should present an idea that is useful but that he should present an idea well."

But we can be sure that this would not have to be said so persistently and so often by some writers if it were not vigorously contradicted by others. In fact, from the other end of the literary world comes a ceaseless protest against the pretension to absolute independence on the part of the artist. For example, when Ernest Psichari

[1] The elements making up this chapter are taken from a conference on " The Responsibility of the Novelist." I would not write about it in quite the same way now. From now henceforward the whole question seems to boil down to the *purification of the source.*

proclaims that one must write with fear and trembling under the eye of the Trinity, he is being the mouthpiece of all those who believe in the immortality of each individual soul, and therefore believe in the extreme importance of their writings as effecting each immortal destiny.

Then, between these two opposing camps, there is the huge crowd of novelists who fluctuate and hesitate. On the one hand they admit that their work is valuable only inasmuch as it apprehends living men in their completeness, in their heights and in their depths—the human creature as he is. They feel that any intervention in the unfolding of their characters—even to prove the truth of what they believe—is an abuse. They feel a sincere revulsion against falsifying life. On the other hand, they know that they are treading on dangerous ground, and that their intense desire to depict human emotions and passions may have an incalculable and permanent effect on the lives of many people.

Every novelist worthy of the name and every playwright who is a born Christian suffers from the torment of this dilemma. In French literature there is a famous example. Once in my holidays I followed the fashion of the time and wrote a life of Jean Racine. Racine is typical of the divided and hesitating writer who plays first into the hands of one camp and then into the hands of the other. The ultimate fate of a writer like him depends on the final decision. Everyone knows what agonizing fluxes Racine went through before he reached that decision. At the age of twenty he escaped from Port-Royal because his young genius revolted against the unbearable restraints imposed upon him there. Then, when Nicole, in his letter on *Les Imaginaires* made a violent attack on novelists and playwrights, Racine burned with rage. Nicole had written that " the qualities of the novelist and the playwright, which anyway are not very honourable in the judgment of decent people, are horrible when considered in the light of the principles of the Christian religion and the rules of the Gospel. Novelists and dramatic poets are public poisoners, not only of the bodies, but the souls of the faithful, and they ought to hold themselves guilty of a multitude of spiritual murders." Racine replied to this hard hitting with unparalleled verve and bitterness and venom in two letters which are not enough known. In our desire to excuse Racine for being unable to endure such inflexible doctrines without an outcry, we must be careful not to blame it on the inhuman rigour of the Jansenists. Nicole was only developing a doctrine of St. Augustine ; and Bossuet showed himself equally uncompromising in his letter to Père Caffaro on the subject of the play and the novel. Bossuet maintained that the success of plays and novels was due to the fact that people find in them substitutes for love and beauty and for their own feelings ; and what answer can be made to that ? The real reason why Racine was so furious with Nicole was because he was hurt to the quick. During the following years we can trace the struggle that he had with himself until finally, at the age of thirty-eight, he gave in and renounced for ever the depicting of human passions and personalities.

It is a renunciation that very few writers are capable of making, and Racine's renunciation was certainly not so easy as some people think. Is a man who is capable of writing and who has a masterpiece inside him at liberty not to give it to the world ? An author who gives up writing may do it because his belly is empty, as the saying goes, and he would only be able to repeat himself and copy himself. Self-repetition, in fact, is the occupation of most writers on the decline ; even when they have given over everything that was expected of them and delivered their message to the world they go on regularly laying eggs because it is their job, and, after all, a man must live.

No human power, however, could reduce a man to silence during his period of fertility ;

there would have to be a supernatural power. We do not know whether Grace has ever been able to triumph over a writer who has writing-sickness. The conversion of a literary man is usually marked by redoubled activity and effort on his part. He wants the greatest possible number of people to read about the example that he gives to the world. We are still awaiting the miracle of a writer who is reduced to silence by God.

Actually, all the best writers are tugging at one rope. At one end of the rope there are those who are convinced that their work will be valuable only if it is disinterested and does not tamper with reality for reasons of modesty or edification, and at the other end there are those who have a feeling of responsibility towards their readers, of whom, in spite of their scruples, they want as large a number as possible. At one end there is the certainty that there cannot be a work in novel-form which has value outside absolute submission to its object—the human heart : there must be progress in knowledge of mankind, but whatever depths are found there must be no dizziness or disgust or horror. This is a certainty. At the other end there is only a sentiment, a feeling—at any rate for those who do not belong to a religious faith. For a Christian, eternity hangs in the balance if one soul is troubled or in danger of being lost. But while non-Christians are unable to stop themselves feeling a responsibility, in a dim way they have no difficulty at all in inventing sophisms to persuade themselves that their fear of scandalising others has no connection with reality. I should like to assure them, at this point, that their nebulous feeling corresponds with a very deep reality. We can say this : that although the whole matter seems more serious for writers with the faith, it certainly does interest the sceptics—and this, precisely because they only believe in man and know no reality in the world other than human reality.

A few years ago a review posed the question : " Why do you write ? " to the literary world. The majority of answerers merely tried to be witty ; Paul Morand, for instance, said : " To be rich and esteemed." He was making fun of the whole thing by confusing immediate motives with deep motives.

The deep motive seems to me to lie in the instinct which urges us not to be alone. A writer is essentially a man who will not be resigned to solitude. Each of us is like a desert, and a literary work is like a cry from the desert, or like a pigeon let loose with a message in its claws, or like a bottle thrown into the sea. The point is : to be heard—even if by one single person.

And the point is that our thoughts and, if we are novelists, our characters should be understood and loved and welcomed by other intelligences and other hearts. An author who assures you that he writes for himself alone and that he does not care whether he is heard or not is a boaster and is deceiving either himself or you. Every man suffers if he is alone, and the artist is the man for whom and in whom this suffering takes a physical form. Baudelaire was right when he called artists *lighthouses*. They light a great fire in the darkness, and they set light to themselves so as to attract the greatest number of their fellow-beings to them.

Artists, and particularly writers, are the most squeamish people in the world, and at the same time the most hungry for praise. Indeed it is impossible for writers to be sated with compliments—and they must not be despised for this because, as often as not, their great need of praise is due to a lack of confidence in themselves, and their longing for reassurance is due to a feeling that their work is worthless.

Of all the compliments that can be paid to a writer, there is one especially that will make him glow with pleasure, namely : " You are admired so much among the younger generation." Then his head positively swells, for though he may seem to be detached, what he wants above all things is to get the attention of the younger generation, and if he does not do this he considers he has failed in his mission. Nothing matters to him except that. He has got to reach others, and particularly he has got to reach those who are still capable of being influenced and dominated, the young mentalities which are hesitating and unformed. He wants to leave his mark on this living wax and imprint all that is best in him on those who are going to survive him. It is not enough for the writer who writes so as not to be alone merely to reach other people : he wants to make them replicas of himself : he wants his own image and likeness to be resurrected in them when he himself is in the grave.

We must not believe in a writer's false humility. The humblest writer aspires to nothing short of immortality, and the least pretentious clings to the hope that he will not perish altogether. Those who pretend that they do not care about what they write and only scribble their poems on cigarette folders do so with a secret hope that because these are lighter they will be carried by the wind to distant shores. The artist wants to escape from his desert during his life, but he also wants to escape from the solitude of death, and thus he hopes that something of what he has written—if only one line—should live, and that some youth—if only one—should hum a song he has invented to the end of the world. The ambition of an artist is not confined to wanting himself to live, but he wants his love to live too. He is audacious enough to impose on men of the future the vision of the face he has loved :

> " Je te donne ces vers afin que si mon nom
> Aborde heureusement aux époques lointaines
> Et fait rêver un soir les cervelles humaines
> Vaisseau favorisé par un grand aquilon . . ."

But if the writer has so great a desire to reach and affect the largest possible quantity of people both in his own time and after it, surely he ought to feel a responsibility towards those he influences, even if he is not a Christian. And even if we abandon the word *responsibility*—which cannot have the same meaning for a sceptic as for a Christian—he still must feel *concerned* for those whose destiny he has perhaps altered.

Actually I know of no writers worthy of the name who are really not concerned—however non-religious they may be. I do not mean that this consideration has an influence on their work or moves them to control either their curiosity or the boldness of their depiction, for they always persuade themselves that a work which is true and in conformity with reality must necessarily be good. Flaubert had no desire for a title to fame other than that of demoralizer, and André Gide, nowadays, would not disown that same title. This does not mean that these writers intend to do evil ; not at all, but they do not agree with us about the nature of good and evil. According to them a work which scandalizes is nearly always a work which sets people free. They see a writer as a sort of satanic benefactor who breaks the bandages of morality in which people are wrapped and restores liberty and ease to their movements. However, this is not the place to point out how these authors are wrong from the Christian point of view—how they do not take the dogma of the Fall of Man into account, nor the fact that man is born defiled, nor the virulent and terribly contagious element in the sores which literature is unveiling with increasing brazenness.

This does not take away from the fact that a novel is nothing if it is not a study of human nature, and that it loses all its reason for existing if it does not increase our knowledge of the human heart. Thus, should a novelist, however scrupulous he may be, falsify the facts of life and change the very object of his study in order not to offend or unsettle his readers ?

I know that the question can be evaded in more ways than one ; but we must not reassure ourselves with the hypocritical excuse that we are not writing for little girls, and are not bound to compete with Mme. de Ségur or Mrs. Moles-

worth. Unfortunately, readers who have attained
the age of reason are often more dangerously dis-
turbed by books than other readers. It is probably better to be read by little girls who have tea
in the nursery and who do not know what evil
is than by young people in full flush of youth.
It would be difficult to imagine the sort of letters
a writer can receive. After reading a book of
mine called *Genetrix*, a boy once sent me a photograph with the words : " To the man who nearly
made me kill my grandmother." In an accom-
panying letter he explained that the old lady
resembled the heroine of *Genetrix* to such an extent
that he had been on the very verge of strangling
her during her sleep. How can readers like that
be protected ? Father Bethléem himself cannot
do anything. The reading of imaginative literature should be forbidden to adults rather than
to children.

It is seldom that writers who distort reality
and depict untrue characters so as to be sure of
not being immoral attain their object. For it
must be remembered that they are not the only
authors of their novels ; the reader himself
collaborates with them and often adds horrors
without their knowing it. We would be amazed
if we knew exactly what happened to our
characters in the imagination of this or that
reader who talks to us about our books. I

think I can say with truth that no book has moved me more deeply than a simple and innocent novel called *Feet of Clay* which I adored when I was fourteen. It was the work of an old and virtuous woman called Zénaïde Fleuriot, and it was full of imagination and sensibility. The heroine had the lovely name of Armelle Trahec. She was young and red-haired with freckles on her face, and since reading about her I have distributed these freckles generously on the faces of my own heroines. Yet when a journalist asks me the names of the writers who have influenced me most, I quote Balzac and Dostoievsky, but I never dare mention Mlle. Zénaïde Fleuriot.

This is a reminder that the devil never loses his rights, and it can well be imagined that on the Day of Judgment, though some writers will have to answer for the souls they have upset, others will be surprised by the unforeseen echo which their simplest works have had in other souls.

The collaboration between the reader and the writer, varying as it does with each individual, makes the question of good and bad books an almost insoluble one. I think that only a novelist is in the position to judge of it. For my own part I know by experience and by confidential admission that the book in which an excessive outspokenness has been detected—and doubtless

rightly—and which has been most severely
censured is also the very book which has had the
greatest effect on people from the religious point
of view. We must not forget that the worst
books as well as the best are double-edged
weapons which the unknown reader plays with
in a way we can never foresee. We cannot
foresee whether the libertine and debauched
element in the reader will be wounded or the
good and pious one. Every human being makes
his honey according to his recipe ; he passes
from book to book and from doctrine to doctrine,
taking what is good for him. The young men
who committed suicide after reading Goethe's
Werther would have finished up by finding,
somewhere else, an excuse for abandoning this
mortal dizziness. Goethe cannot be held responsible for the death. Everybody re-creates what
he reads after his own heart's-image, and moulds
an idea of it which is valid for himself alone.
I suppose it is my own peculiar feeling, but what
stands out most vividly for me in the colossal
and putrescent work of Proust is the image of a
gaping hole, the sensation of infinite absence,
and it is this chasm and emptiness—the absence
of God in fact—which strikes me most about
mankind according to Proust. I see this because
I am a Christian ; others may very well find
satisfaction in these gloomiest of pictures. And

that is why wretched literary people can still
hope that the evil they have done will be forgiven
because of the good which—often unknowingly
—they have also done.

That is how I reassured myself. But sincerity
with regard to oneself is the virtue of our generation, so we should be bold and face up to our
vices. All I have said does not prevent our con-
senting to the professional depiction of human
passions. Human passions are the object of our
study, and we sell our books solely because
thousands of people experience a kind of uneasy
delight in this depiction of them. St. Augustine
confesses that he found in plays " the image of
his miseries, the love and the food of his fire . . ."
However, there is absolutely no need to write
about obscenity in order to spread fire in the
world. Bossuet said : " Do you not feel that
there are things which have no very specific
effect, but which, without seeming harmful at
first, put evil tendencies and dispositions into
people's minds ? Everything that provides food
for the passions is of this dim origin. There
would be only too much to confess if one examined
oneself to find the causes of sin." And he adds :
" If anyone could discern in a man a certain
depth of sensual joy, and certain restless vague
disposition for indulging the pleasures of the
senses—tending nowhere and yet tending every-

where—he would know the secret source of the greatest sins."

Can we honestly deny that it is nearly always this " secret source of the greatest sins " which is probed by the writer? I am not saying that he does it on purpose or as the result of long premeditation. But in the light of this quotation from Bossuet we can understand better what André Gide means when he says that no work of art can come into being without the collaboration of the devil. The writer depends on this " depth of sensual joy " in order to absorb and move his readers ; he depends on this " vague and restless disposition for indulging the pleasures of the senses—tending nowhere and yet tending everywhere." The writer keeps up collusion with his adversary, the reader, whereas he ought to conquer him at any price. In every man—especially in every young man—and in every woman he has an accomplice personifying a desire for languor, a taste for emotion and a thirst for tears. Once again, I do not think there is a single novelist worthy of the name who thinks of that while he is writing and who deliberately sets out to upset people, but he is spurred on by sure instinct. All his art is concentrated on reaching the secret source of the greatest sins, and the more genius he has the more surely he will reach his end.

This question then emerges : Must one stop writing even if one feels deeply that writing is one's vocation and that literary creation is as natural as breathing ? Perhaps some doctor holds the key to the enigma ; perhaps somebody somewhere knows the way in which a scrupulous novelist can escape from these choices—these three choices of either changing the object of his observation or falsifying life or running the risk of spreading scandal and misery among his fellow-creatures.

We may as well admit that a writer who is torn by this problem is hardly ever taken seriously. On his left there is only mockery and shrugging of shoulders—a refusal to admit that such a problem really exists. People deny that an artist has any other duty than to realise and achieve a beautiful piece of work, or that he can have any other care than to approach as near as possible to psychological truth. On his right there is an even greater misunderstanding. There is a total ignorance of the fact that he has scruples or high motives at all. It is difficult not to have a choking feeling the first time pious reviewers treat you as a pornographer and accuse you of writing obscenity for the sake of making money. When I was young and naive I felt an insuperable desire to pour out my heart to some distinguished and holy people about all

73

these difficulties, but as soon as I had begun I realised that they made no essential distinction between me and, for instance, the author of the *Revue des Folies-Bergères*. I am not really shocked by their attitude, for I can understand perfectly well that people who are specifically in charge of souls are faced with an infinite number of problems which are far more urgent to them than the æsthetic problem, and it would be ludicrous for me to feel indignant with them on the grounds that they do not consider æsthetics to be as important as I do.

One Catholic writer has realised the importance of this problem and made a real effort to solve it. I could not follow Jacques Maritain's train of thought in all its complexity, but I shall quote a few lines taken from *Art and Scholasticism* in which he delimits very exactly the sphere of the novelist who is worried by his responsibility. " The essential point," he says, " is not to know whether a novelist may or may not portray a given aspect of evil. The essential point is to know at what altitude he is when he makes this portrayal and whether his art and his soul are pure enough and strong enough to make it without conniving with it. The more the modern novel plunges into human misery, the more are superhuman virtues demanded from the novelist. For example, to write the work of a Proust as it should be written would require the interior light of a Saint Augustine. Unfortunately, it is just the opposite that has happened, and we see the observer and the thing observed—the novelist and his subject—rivalling one another in degradation."

This is what Jacques Maritain says, and everyone will agree that he puts the question very well ; everyone, that is, except the novelists.[1] However, he does not take into account the real point, since he neglects to consider the fundamental laws of novel-creation. He mentions the " observer and the thing observed." In fact he

[1] Since I wrote this, Jacques Maritain has replied to me in the Roseau d'Or (No. 30) : " Does it mean that, in my opinion, the novelist ought to cut himself off from his characters and observe them from outside in the way a scientist in his laboratory follows the experiments he has set going ? No, of course not. Would the character exist if he did not live in the author and the author did not live in him ? It is not in virtue of a simple metamorphosis, but rather in virtue of a deep analogy, that it is proper to place the art of the novel in the theological light of the mystery of creation properly speaking."

And further on : " The part of the novelist is not that of the scientist. The scientist is only responsible for notions, is only concerned with truth. He only addresses himself to a limited public of specialised readers.

" The novelist is answerable for an almost unlimited influence. Only rarely do his readers consist of those for whom his message is made (who are probably few in number). He knows that. He bewails it. He profits by it. The *unlimited* nature of his public makes the problem more and more difficult. . . ."

Further on Maritain denounces me for a tendency to Manichæism, and writes : " The Blood of the redemption, which can turn a man into a friend of God, can also, if It touches them, exorcise Art and the Novel."

I am aware to-day of how much I owe to the deep charity which Maritain has shown to me in these pages of the Roseau d'Or."

compares a novelist bending over the human heart with a physiologist bending over a frog or a guinea-pig. According to Maritain, the novelist is detached from his subject in the way the man in the laboratory is detached from the animal whose stomach he is delicately dissecting. I, however, hold that the operation of the novelist is utterly different from that of the experimentalist. As far as the novel is concerned, Jacques Maritain has stopped at the old naturalistic ideas. It is a condition of art that the novelist should connive with the subject of his creation, in spite of Maritain's warning, for the real novelist is not an observer, but a creator of fictitious life. It is not his function to observe life, but to create it. He brings living people into the world ; he does not observe them from some lofty vantage point. He even confuses and, in a way, loses his own personality in the subject of his creation. He is one with his creation, and his identification with it is pushed so far that he actually becomes his creation.

It could easily be argued that if a novelist keeps the superhuman virtues that Maritain would have him keep, he could never write about evil people. His characters could not be wicked if they came from a creator who was good and pure. A good tree does not yield bad fruit. Let the novelist busy himself with his personal

76

sanctification and nothing scandalous can emerge from his mind. True though this may be, it is worth mentioning in passing that the practice of superhuman virtue is not easy for mankind in general nor for novelists in particular. In that case, would not a deeply virtuous man refrain from writing novels? For if he is a real artist he will not feel capable of producing insipid though edifying stories without a trace of human truth in them, and at the same time he will know very well that a living piece of work is bound to cause trouble. It is probably true that a novelist subconsciously resurrects in his characters the desires which he himself has repressed, and the temptations which he himself has overcome; thus, just as admirable men often have unworthy sons, the best novelist may find that he has re-incarnated his own worst elements in the sons and daughters of his brain. That is why a fervent Christian feels justified in describing passions from " on high "—for example in a sermon or a treatise—whereas he does not in a novel where it is not so much a question of judging and condemning them as of giving them flesh and blood. Nothing, as we know, can prevent a fire from burning. Henri Perreyve, when he had just left school, wrote a letter to Charles Perraud in which he referred to " this vice of lustfulness which word alone makes our seventeen-year-old hearts grow weak and faint." If the mere mention of the word makes these young people grow faint and weak, what can be the effect of descriptions of the word—even if they are restrained descriptions?

Somebody may say that vice is not the only thing to write about, and that though man has his rottenness he also has his greatness ; there are beautiful characters whose history can be written. Indeed, I am far from sharing Gide's opinion that good literature cannot be made out of fine sentiments, and that the worse the characters are the better the book. Nevertheless, it certainly is not easy to make good literature with only good sentiments, and it is almost impossible to isolate the good from the bad so as to make an edifying portrayal. The ambition of the modern novelist is to apprehend the whole of human nature, including its shifting contradictions. In the world of reality you do not find beautiful souls in the pure state—these are only to be found in novels and in bad novels at that. What we call a beautiful character has become beautiful at the cost of a struggle against itself, and this struggle should not stop until the bitter end. The evil which the beautiful character has to overcome in itself and from which it has to sever itself, is a reality which the novelist must account for. If there is a reason for the existence of the novelist on earth it is this : to show the element which holds out against God in the highest and noblest characters—the innermost evils and dissimulations ; and also to light up the secret source of sanctity in creatures who seem to us to have failed.

Some people, however, have succeeded in overcoming their natures. The saints form material for novelists as much as any other living people. Why should not we portray saints just as Benson, Foggaro, Boumann and Bernanos did —or tried to do ? On the other hand it could be maintained that on this very point of sanctity the novelist loses his rights, for if he tries to write a novel about sanctity he is no longer dealing purely with men, but with the action of God on men—and this may be an extremely unwise thing to try to do. On this point it seems that the novelist will always be beaten by reality, by the saints who really have lived. St. Francis of Assisi, St. Catherine of Siena, the big and little St. Theresa and all the great mystics, are witnesses to a reality and an experience which is infinitely beyond the power of a novelist.

Whenever a novelist has tried to re-create the way of grace, with all its struggles and its ultimate victory, he has left an impression of arbitrariness and misrepresentation. Nothing is more elusive in human life than the finger of

79

God. It is not that it is not visible, but its imprint is so delicate that it disappears as soon as we try to capture it. God is inimitable, and He escapes the novelist's grasp. I am sure that the exceptional success of Bernanos' novel, *Sous le soleil de Satan*, is due precisely to the fact that its saint is not a real saint : this tormented and agonized hero wanders too near the edge of despair. Or suppose, if you like, that the hero, Abbé Donissan, is a real saint ; then Bernanos, with his novelist's instinct, meets that supposition by finally discovering in him the secret failure and deviation which, in spite of his heroic virtues, relates him to sinful humanity. The reason why most novelists have failed in their portrayal of saints may be due to the fact that they have drawn creatures who are sublime and angelic but not human, whereas their sole chance of success would have lain in concentrating on the wretched and human elements in their characters that sanctity allows to subsist. And this is the special realm of the novelist.

When I read the lives of the great saints I was always worried by their manifestations of humility, which seemed to me excessive. It seemed to me that people at such a height of perfection and practising such heroic virtues could not have been absolutely sincere when they announced how wretched and unworthy they were and strived to debase themselves below everyone else. But now I am convinced that sanctity means, above all, lucidity. " One must know oneself to the pitch of being horrified," Bossuet wrote to the Maréchal de Bellefonds. As the saints advance in the double knowledge of God and of their own souls, they get such a piercing vision of their unworthiness that they abase themselves and annihilate themselves by the most natural of instincts. It is not enough to say that they believe themselves to be wretched : in fact they *are* wretched, and it is precisely their sanctity that makes them see it so lucidly. They see what man, as compared with the light of God, really is even when sanctified, and they are horrified.

Thus even if a novelist devoted himself entirely to depicting the souls of saints, he would finally get back to the human—that is, the dangerous—element in man. He could not avoid the abysses lying in his way. There is often a sort of vanquished and frustrated viciousness at the source of people's lives. This has been said about some great revolutionaries and some great heretics, but it is equally true of very good and holy men.

Thus it happens that the novelist, caught between two fires as he is with all these difficulties, sometimes experiences a temptation to which, I must admit, he very rarely yields : the temptation

to be silent—to be silent, to finish with these
heavy and gloomy disclosures, to refrain from
presenting the world with creatures who are
diseased and who spread their disease, to make
the sacrifice that Jean Racine made and which
we admire so much.

Bossuet said that there was no greater difference
than the difference between living according to
nature and living according to grace. If the
novelist is religious he suffers from this divergence,
which upsets all Christians, in an especially sharp
and tragic way. How could he consent to
silence ? And if he cannot come to a solution on
this point we must remember to take into account
the poor and sordid motives which attach a man
to his job—especially when his job, as with the
job of literature, flatters his vanity and his liking
for a halo and at the same time brings him various
sorts of advantages. But the necessity which
obliges a genuine man of letters to write must not
be forgotten. He cannot not write. He follows
a deep and imperative need. We cannot smother
the restless and importunate germs inside us ;
they demand life and we cannot know beforehand
what sort of souls they will have. Our sincerest
critics ought to ponder and try to understand
Goncourt's affirmation : " One does not write
the book one wants to." No, we do not write the
book we want to write ; alas, we write the book

we deserve to write. Our judges come down on us as though our work were entirely dependent on our own free will, as if we made a deliberate decision to write a good or a bad book, tell an edifying story or a scandalous one. They do not seem to have the remotest idea of the mysterious unforeseeable and inevitable element in all creative novel-writing. The urge to write in a man of letters ends up by becoming a monster-like necessity which cannot be frustrated. Some time ago there was an amusing drawing that a hat manufacturer used as an advertisement : it consisted of a machine with a live rabbit going into it at one end and hats coming out of it at the other. It is like this that life, with all its hopes and sorrows, is engulfed by the novelist, and nothing can prevent a book emerging from this perpetual receiving of impressions. Even if he withdraws from the world and shuts his eyes and stops up his ears, his most distant past will begin to ferment. His childhood and youth alone is enough to provide a born novelist with an immense amount of literary nourishment. Nobody can stop the flow of the river which flows from us.

There is no doubt that our books have a deep resemblance to ourselves, and we can quite rightly be judged and condemned by them. Novalis' axiom, " Character is destiny," has often been repeated. And so, just as there is a close bond between a man's character and what happens to him during his life, so there is a similar relationship between a novelist's character and the creatures and events brought into being by his imagination. This is not to say that he is any more the absolute master of these creatures and events than he is of the course of his own fate.

People of my calibre complicate the " drama of the Catholic novelist." The humblest priest would tell me, like Maritain : " Be pure, become pure, and your work too will have a reflection in heaven. Begin by purifying the source and those who drink of the water cannot be sick . . ." And I give the last word to the priest.

CHAPTER VI

IT occurs to me to wonder whether this book is as sincere as I meant it to be. In re-reading it I detect a desire to complicate a very ordinary case in the way that a fish churns the water so as to escape. Why should I seek so far afield? If a man is born in Christianity he has not got to discover it but to recover it. It is like a river that has been dammed. The difficulties I am dealing with tend to make me forget the facilities that result from long familiarity with religion. Probably a man who is making the first steps in spiritual life and who has never knelt down and never talked to God will envy me my childhood habits, which I have the cheek to groan at, and the familiarity with the things of heaven.

One thing is certain, and that is that there is no lie in this book with regard to the irritation of a soul which is drawn to God as inevitably as a plant to the sun, and a plant, moreover, which has the power of resisting its own special law. I wonder what the origin of this resistance and this refusal is? When the time comes for a man to see the truth clearly, the truth outside which there cannot be even temporal salvation for him, nothing is simpler than that he should follow his path, give himself over, slide into submission, shut his eyes and, like a child, surrender himself to Almighty God.

To understand the temptation that a soul undergoes at God's hands and the desperate evasiveness that it attempts when surrounded by grace, you must remember the astonishment I felt when I studied the life of Jean Racine. In my opinion the mystery of Jean Racine is his perseverance. I was not surprised by his sudden change in the year he wrote *Phèdre*, a change which might have been provoked by any one of the thousands of causes that are the historian's domain. But what passed my comprehension was the fact that he did not falter until his death, and more than that, he became further and further involved in the spiritual life.

All the time that this man whose vicissitudes I am describing was estranged from God, Christ had a continual magnetism for him, and also a prestige which seemed to grow in inverse proportion to the distance which separated him from it. For there is an essential difference between the Christian who resists the life of Grace—that is to say, the sinner—and the religionless man who gives in to the corruption of his nature. The latter thinks he can put corruption inside borders

86

and integrate it into a normal and honourable
worldly life. But the sinner knows with a knowledge that comes from God that he will not have
done anything towards his salvation if he does
not cut off the growth of evil at the root and kill
it at the heart. The man who is without God
never dreams of so much as envisaging this, since
the whole thing appears quite absurd to him and
quite beyond the scope of man. But the sinner
is aware that it is possible, he is aware that God
gives renewed strength each day, so much so that
compared with the thousands of spiritual resurrec-
tions achieved by Grace each moment, he sees
the resurrection of Lazarus as a very commonplace miracle.

Seen from afar, this total renewal is by no
means repugnant to the sinner. Every man has
felt at least once the desire to start out afresh
and begin life all over again. What flesh and
blood has not burned with desire to be washed
from impurity? And although the Church
demands that we should hate our sins and be
sorry for them, it does not want us to be weighed
down by them. The mysterious wisdom of the
Church demands of us both expiation and
forgetfulness.

In one of the public letters which Gide has
done me the questionable honour of sending me,
he says he is shocked because one of his friends

felt nothing but joy at his conversion and forbade himself be sorry about a past which he said he wanted to forget.[1] I can quite believe that his friend expressed these feelings to Gide, but I am certain that he never meant that he would have nothing more to do with repentance. Repentance is the natural state of the converted sinner : but this state does not necessitate a perpetual review of past delinquencies. Obsessions and scruples lead to *delectatio morosa* ; they retard the soul in its progress and interrupt spiritual advance.

I think the most powerful inducement to return to God is the attractiveness of making a break

[1] " My dear Mauriac,
      " I must protest—with friendship but with force—against the way you have misunderstood my meaning. I wrote the lines which you refer to after a conversation with Ghéon who had just become a Catholic. We were talking about repentance and contrition, and he told me with feeling that his zeal and love for Christ were so great that he could only feel deep joy. He said it was enough to hate sin and to hate everything that deflected him from Christ, and that he could never bring himself to feel contrite about things he had done in his past because that necessitated looking back into a past which he wanted to forget and make non-existent.
      " And it was at this point, in thinking of this man who had been my greatest friend, that I suddenly understood the words of Christ. It seemed to me impossible that anyone who believed implicitly in the gospel should believe that a disavowal of one's sins was sufficient without a profound repentance for them. And is not that precisely what Christ meant when He said : ' Whoever does not lift up his cross and follow Me is not worthy of Me.' This is to say : ' Whoever presumes to follow Me without having previously lifted up his cross . . .' And this made me think of the mistake that most translators make, and made me decide always to follow the Vulgate. The idea of identification with the Cross to the pitch of abuse, and the idea of transforming an instrument of pain into a luxurious pillow simply had not entered my head.

                                                    " André Gide."

88

in one's life and, as they say, changing one's
skin and becoming another person. And the
power of this inducement increases at certain
times—with the disgust for sin, for example, and
the sorrow sin begets ; in fact, when this world
shows too plainly its criminal habit of ceasing to
be pleasant. A sinner may yield to this inducement once, twice, an incalculable number of
times, and this means that not one of his returns
to God was binding, that he lacked perseverance
to such an extent that he was unable to believe
that the grace of perseverance had ever been
given him.

He has hardly savoured the charm of the
Christian life, the happiness of being delivered
of his burden and the belief that he is worthy of
resting in the peace and joy of Christ, when
there looms on the horizon the unexpected and
brutally powerful army of assault which the enemy
has been holding in reserve for that very moment.
He sees the thousand intellectual objections and
all the difficulties of belief which the real sinner
has never had the time nor the inclination to
dream of.

He is assailed all at once by everything which
the human intelligence can construe and hurl
against Catholic dogma, and at the point where
his defence is worst prepared. Then the voice
of the tempter is heard : " What ? Are you

sacrificing the joys of the heart, the caresses and repose of the flesh, for this old metaphysic founded on an utterly outworn and superseded system of physics ? Are you embarking on this old ship which has been abandoned by nearly everybody of any importance in the human race, deserted by the philosophers, the writers, the leaders and the rank-and-file ? You are choosing the moment when it is leaking to book your passage and you will throw untold wealth into the sea. Look around you : you are alone." And just as the enemy is speaking, forgotten lusts and desires poke up their faces again, filled with a new mystery. One by one the passions awake, prowl around and sniff at the object of their covetousness ; they are attacking the poor undecided soul from the back and he is done for. How often has he got to be hurled into the ditch, to be stifled by the mud, to grasp at the edges and arise to the light again, to feel his hands give way and return again to the darkness, before he finally submits to the law of the spiritual life— the least understood law in the world and the one that repels him most, and yet without it he cannot attain the grace of perseverance. What is required is the renunciation of the ego, and this is expressed perfectly in the phrase of Pascal: "Entire and sweet renunciation. Absolute submission to Jesus Christ and to my spiritual director."

People may laugh at this and scoff at you for being unworthy of the title of free man and for having to submit yourself to a master, and, what is more, not merely an external sort of master who can break the arm of Epictetus while remaining powerless over his soul, but a master who brings our very thoughts and desires, before we know them ourselves, into subjection.

But this enslavement is really a miraculous liberation, for even when you were free you spent the whole time forging chains for yourself and putting them on, riveting them tighter and tighter each moment. During the years when you thought you were free you submitted like an ox to the yoke to your countless hereditary ills. From the hour of your birth not one of your crimes has failed to go on living, has failed to imprison you more and more every day, has failed to beget other crimes. The Man you submit yourself to *does not want you to be free to be a slave :* he breaks the vicious circle of your fetters, and, against your half-extinguished and still-smouldering desires, He kindles and re-kindles the fire of Grace, for, as St. Paul wrote to the Hebrews, " Our God is also a devouring fire."

CHAPTER VII

THE greatest agony a man can experience is to survey his past from middle age and to realise that he has not been the master of his own life. When he is ageing, all the hidden interior enemies that have forced him to do certain things, remove their disguises. The huge rugged marks of fate stand out in the web of the past. There is a terrible repetition about the things he has done, the things he has not done, the things he could not help doing—they are over and done with, and yet they are ever-present and somehow perpetuated in the way the features of a horrible grandfather are reproduced in the grandchild. The crime he committed last night recalls feature by feature the crime committed twenty years ago, and the sin he has just committed will beget the sin of the day after to-morrow.

It is a tightly woven web, and no power in the world can interrupt the unrolling of it, and no scene of the drama it unweaves can be detached or put aside.

It is a fatal interdependence, and however far back into remote childhood he may go, he will find that the features are there, the wrinkles are there which mar his face at the age of forty and which he sees in the mirror with fear and horror.

There were presages of all the pain to come in childish misadventures in the playground. Even before his heart had quickened, before it had felt the breathless pulsations of love, it was an empty space where indistinct forms stretched out feelers, where passions were larvæ and sufferings and crimes were chrysalises, sleeping unknowingly.

And if he wishes to go further back than childhood and reach the very source of his fate, he may see it leaping from the womb of the earth, poisoned even then with all the substances which poison it to-day. It springs up from the country cemetery and from the bones which, in days gone by, made secret acts like the secret acts which he himself is enjoying to-day. If inanimate objects in houses where the furniture is never moved could see and remember things, I am sure that every couch on which living bodies are outstretched from generation to generation would recognize, after half a century, the same aberrations, embraces and follies.

At this moment, when surveying the fatality and implacable continuity of his past life, he cannot be deluded into thinking that his declining years will be any different in character from the years he has already lived. Adolescence was contained in potency in his childhood and his childhood in his infancy and in the same way his spattered maturity holds all the elements of a shameful old-age. The future old man is present in this baldness and this shapeless mouth, and he is still more present in this soul which becomes increasingly enslaved every day to the habits which time first strengthens and then makes insurmountable. The stakes are made, and they have been made ever since his birth : even before his birth the stakes were made.

Then he lifts his head, defies despair and settles down to worship his life. In order to do this he puts it in shape, for even if his will cannot create what does not exist nor stop the existence of what does exist, it can at least make use of the elements that fate has put at its disposal and piece them together in an order that is satisfying to his taste. In this way æsthetics become confused with ethics, and his object is to formulate an artistic theory of submission to his own particular instincts.

He no longer, therefore, seeks the outer darkness so as to submit himself to the laws of his flesh, but he lifts his arms and shakes the chains on his wrists joyfully, glorying in them and encouraging other enchained people to do the same. He professes that the law written in his innermost heart comes from God, and he professes it with the very authority which allowed him to deny the divine origin of the holy tribunal of conscience. Is, or is not, a sin something that one cannot help committing? " Look ! " he says, " Look at me. I have not any troubles or worries or uneasiness and I shall always laugh at people who have. I can laugh ; and at the age of sixty I can have a second childhood that will make all my generation admire me ! "

" I am not worried." Why this need to reiterate what ought to be taken for granted ? If everything is already designed and arranged, and if it is only in my capacity as writer that I can interfere with the organisation of my life, I can surely only feel relief and ease—unless I feel despair ; but complete despair is only another way of expressing calmness and peace.

Nevertheless, is there a man on earth who does not feel uneasiness and agitation ? You, who make fun of mine, you have your own. You are a writer which means that you hand yourself over at every moment of the day and night. There is not anything in you that we do not know, and the very fact that you boast so vigorously about your lack of anguish shows that this lack must be a new thing with you. And you know how precarious it is better than we do.

The features of your life are designed and flow

onwards in an interrupted order and movement
—to-day's were embryonic in yesterday's. But
in spite of this you always seem to think that
these features could be altered and that the
flow could at least be turned aside and given a
new direction if not altogether stopped. Sometimes you have hoped for an intervention from
the outside, and sometimes you have feared one,
but whether fearful or hopeful you have always
thought it possible to have one. *Everyone of us
awaits the hour when he will see, not the expected face
on the web of his past, but an unknown face—agoniz-
ingly sweet and covered with blood.*

In the same sovereign way with which His
incarnation breaks the barriers of history, Jesus
Christ can choose the favourable moment to
come into our lives and unite Himself with the
stream of each particular destiny. He wants to
introduce His will into this apparent fatality to
destroy its fatality. Sometimes these attempts are
hidden, like " asides," with long intervals before
renewal, but often they are direct and imperious
and pressing like a unique and important occasion. However enslaved a man may feel, these
attempts always give him the feeling that he has
the power to say " yes " or " no." At the
approach of a familiar temptation he may
believe that no force in the world could prevent
him from giving in to it, and that a determination

not to give in to it would be absolutely beyond his powers. But faced with the approach of God, *which demands that he should be weak*, he suddenly feels himself terrifyingly free. He is a slave when confronted with an occasion of sin, but he is free when confronted with Someone who demands that he shall be weak, that he shall show acceptance and abandonment. It is nothing more or less than a demand that he shall consent not to defend himself, not to put himself in opposition, in fact, to play the part of a dead man.

People will say that they have not ever felt the exigence of this unknown stream, wanting to enter into their lives and swell them with its own waters. They say that there are religious temperaments and non-religious temperaments, and that neither will ever convince the other.

Nevertheless, if we had the power of comprehending the most secret currents of each man's life, I am sure we should discover the place where the appeal had struck a chord. And again, many obviously religious characters who are carried away by any sort of mysticism often resist and persecute Christ. We see intellectuals joining Him in the name of reason, and they are not moved by the " reasons of the heart " until after their conversion. In this both kinds of mind submit to or resist Grace in different ways. Just as much as the intellect, the heart can find pretexts for saying " No " to Christ. At first the heart seems the easiest to convince, but the fact that it can quickly embrace religion means equally that it can quickly reject it and be disgusted by it.

We must admit that a certain brand of intellectualism involves a preliminary rejection and refusal of Grace. Refusals and denials barricade all the entrances that Grace might find, and they break the bridges and block the channels. It seems impossible to conceive of Grace finding an entry into some of the finest minds of France, because they have taken such careful precautions against it. But Grace has more contrivances than we know of.

But in spite of everything, these two kinds of character are separated from each other by an eternal contradiction. They, on their side, say to us that Christ is a fact, that His survival in the world is a fact, that human conscience is a fact, but they think that our thirst for the supernatural prevents us from observing these facts with the necessary detachment. We reply that their passionate denial of the supernatural deprives them of the qualities that such an observation requires.

The suggestion that we should make the whole world problem a mechanical one and approach

the history of religions with this initial prejudice
seems to me laughable. But they on their side
deny that there is any value in the conclusions of
people who throw themselves into the arms of
the gospels. They think that the very fact that
we hunger and thirst for the Absolute is ample
reason for our inventing the God we thirst for.

Our objection is that their refusal always
covers up a selfishness. They put themselves
first, and they reject their own particular cross
rather than the Cross of Christ : they are incapable of renunciation themselves so they renounce
the Christ who would force it on them. They
have to gratify their passions, and so they have
to deny that Christ is the Messiah. They protest
that true courage lies in the ordered and reason-
able gratification of their inclinations, and that
the distinction between good and evil makes life
barren and anæmic. Christians are apparently
afraid of life and cannot appreciate its agonizing
or ecstatic disorders ; thus they have to comfort
themselves with eternal promises.

No argument is more exasperating to a Christian consciousness than this one. The fact is
that on this point our adversaries fall a prey to
a weakness which we all share when face to face
with a doctrine we detest : that of judging it
by its more mediocre expression so that we can
despise it more easily. In reality, the people who

look for comfort and consolation and ease in their religion clutter up the threshold without entering the building. For those who understand it and love it, the spiritual life may be said to be a terrific and terrifying adventure. There can be no playing with the cross. It demands of us things we are unaware of ; it is such a burning passion that it makes the little follies of man appear almost ludicrous. St. John of the Cross said that each one of us would finally be judged on love, and we know where this belief has led the saints. If a man says with Pascal, " Lord, I give You everything," and in a tone that really commits him, his friends can expect or fear anything from him save that he will turn his life into a farce.

But his opponent will never let the Christian have the last word. There is endless misunderstanding and interminable discussion. There would not be any point in carrying the argument further. The Christian has usually been convinced by something which is valid for him alone, If he speaks of an interior influence by which he regained a forgotten love and longing, or if he speaks of a living silence, it is objected that the influence and silence are his own creations because his weakened heart needs them to take breath. There is no bureau of information for spiritual miracles like the one at Lourdes, where physical cures are studied and approved by specialists. Even if the spiritual change which people undergo is visible to the world, it does not appear final or striking in the way that a reabsorbed cancer does. Those who have experienced a spiritual miracle always cling tremblingly to the wretchedness from which Divine mercy redeemed them.

They tremble, but all the same their evidence has been accumulating for a quarter of a century and is in harmony with the deep peace they enjoy, though at the same time they feel a terror of losing it. They say that Grace is tangible, though they know they will not be believed. One of these people who had experienced a spiritual miracle told me that for years he had lived only for the short interviews he was allowed with Grace each week ; not that he was happy in the presence of Grace, but simply that he no longer suffered. All the rest of the time was misery and blind discomfort. He quite realised that his desires exceeded all bounds, for we cannot ask anyone to be always corporeally beside us. He told me that he felt that he had no hope of ever satisfying his craving ; and though he had hoped that time would cure his obsession, he had found that on the contrary it strengthened it and enriched it with daily sorrows until it assumed a relentlessly eternal form. Though he was a great worker, the days seemed to him interminable because they were horribly empty of the one thing he needed. Time had become for him an executioner, and he could not have killed it however hard he tried. He had done any amount of things to fill the yawning gaps left by Grace's non-presence. Perhaps in his view everything that filled this abyss was good. However carnal love may be, it is rarely this that dishonours man but the substitute with which he replaces it. He finds substitutes for it until the day that he discovers that this love itself has usurped a place destined for Another.

This man who has been cured by a miracle—if I have rightly interpreted what he confessed—now rests his faith on a rigorous conformity between his desire and the God whom he possesses. The little image of flesh and blood created in the Divine likeness has fallen suddenly like a mask, and the real Face has appeared, with the real Flesh and the real Blood.

This is the tangible miracle he described to me. After an interior tumult which makes a soul mad for years, there was a prodigious silence, a supernatural calm and a peace beyond all peace. The soul is no longer alone, no longer expects someone, not because it does not love any more, but because its love is carried away by prayer as a lamb is carried away by an eagle.

As the lamb and the eagle soar upwards with the light, unknown and unsuspected reasons for their meeting are discovered. Finally the hope of never being separated begins to awake—a hope so lovely that the heart cannot look at it face to face. In this sense it is absurd to say that God demands that only He should be loved. What He asks is that His love should contain all others.

To this I raised the objection that the spirit cannot be delimited, that our body seeks a like-ness of its own, and that not finding it in the spiritual marriage it makes trouble. It is here that this dead weight can become so living and exigent, like a beast of prey on its own account ; and this objection leads me to talk to this man of the Eucharist.

My instinctive Jansenism always stopped me from seeing why frequent Communion is neces-sary, above all for those of fiery character. The Real Presence, he said, is the real occupation of our flesh, the guarding of the gates and the watch-ing of all the weak points. The Presence which is madly desired by a creature is at last obtained. According to my interlocutor it is not a question of emotional weakness ; no, it is simply that someone is there who fills the role of a creature and who, moreover, carries on his life—he reads, works and chats with a friend. But even in the gaiety of the world a moment of recollection is enough. It is like a hand furtively pushing, a burning breath, and in the midst of the crowd a quick glance of a love that the others are blind to. It is a sign of connivance, a miraculous security.

" Who was it who dared to say that Christianity played no part in the flesh ? " he asked me. I was ashamed to remind him that it was myself, and could only hang my head.